Under the Sunday Tree

They walk together
on Sundays
move slowly
through the park
always remembering
to stop awhile
at the place where
two trees arch as one
leaves touching
like family

Eloise Greenfield

Little People™ Big Book

About
FAMILIES

TIME LIFE for Children™

ALEXANDRIA, VIRGINIA

Table of Contents

A Family Together

Our Family Tree
by H. L. Ross

My name is Betsy M. McBain.
I live at 19 Oak Tree Lane.
In our front yard there stands a tree
Planted early in the century
By Great-Great-Grandpa Jim McBain
Who built this house on Oak Tree Lane.
The bedroom that belongs to me
Was once Great-Grandpa's nursery.
Yes, other families move away
But we McBains just stay and stay.
Our roots run deep; it seems that we
Are planted here, just like this tree.

When Great-Grandpa was only ten
Life wasn't all that easy then;
A big deal just to get a drink
You pumped the water from the sink.
The telephone was on the wall.
You cranked it up to make a call.
From the coalbin black as night
Came coal to keep the stove alight.
The iceman came with ice in blocks
To put into the old icebox;
In those days, that was all they had
To keep fresh things from going bad.

But life was also kind of neat
Fresh ice cream was a special treat.
Dolls were dainty as can be.
The girls back then would serve them tea.
Boys played a game with sticks and hoops
And rode around in noisy groups—
Each on a kind of three-wheeled bike
That looked like a gigantic trike.
The parlor was a place to sit
To embroider or to knit.
The front door had a big brass knocker.
The porch, a wicker sliding rocker.

Grandpa's boyhood days were slower,
They cut the grass with a hand-pushed mower.
They sewed their clothes on pedal Singers,
Wrung their wet wash out in wringers.
Didn't have TV and so
Evenings listened to radio.
Floors were cleaned with broom and mop.
Hand tools were used in the woodwork shop.
Great-Grandma baked pies and cookies galore.
Grandpa ran errands to the store.
His sister's favorite toy of all
Was a set of jacks and a rubber ball.

Yes, other families move away
But we McBains just stay and stay.
Our roots run deep; it seems that we
Are planted here, just like this tree.

Are you wondering what *we're* like?
That's me there riding that pink bike.
That's Jim, my brother, the skateboard pro.
That's Mom who likes to paint and sew.
That's Dad—his hobby is making models—
Antique cars and ships in bottles.
That's my other brother Bret
Who tapes home movies on cassette.
We watch them on our VCR.
I play that I'm a movie star.
The days speed by, they go so fast
Was life *so* different in the past?

Yes, other families move away
But we McBains just stay and stay.
Our roots run deep; it seems that we
Are planted here, just like this tree.

Now take a walk back through time
with the McBain family. Look at the
house in all the pictures. What has
changed? What has stayed the same?
Look at the lights in the house. Look
at the kitchen. Do you see the picture
of Betsy's great-grandmother?
Can you see when it was taken?

Parents

Andre

I had a dream last night. I dreamed
I had to pick a Mother out.
I had to choose a Father too.
At first, I wondered what to do,
There were so many there, it seemed,
Short and tall and thin and stout.

But just before I sprang awake,
I knew what parents I would take.

And *this* surprised and made me glad:
They were the ones I always had!

Gwendolyn Brooks

Over in the Meadow

Traditional Counting Rhyme

Over in the meadow
In the sand, in the sun
Lived an old mother turtle
And her little turtle one.

"Dig!" said the mother.
"I dig," said the one.
And they dug all day
In the sand, in the sun.

Over in the meadow
Where the stream runs blue
Lived an old mother fish
And her little fishes two.

"Swim!" said the mother.
"We swim," said the two.
And they swam all day
Where the stream runs blue.

Over in the meadow
In a hole in a tree
Lived an old mother rabbit
And her little rabbits three.

"Hop!" said the mother.
"We hop," said the three.
And they hopped all day
Near the hole in the tree.

Over in the meadow
In the reeds near the shore
Lived an old mother duck
And her little ducklings four.

"Quack!" said the mother.
"We quack," said the four.
And they quacked all day
In the reeds near the shore.

Over in the meadow
In a snug beehive
Lived a mother bumblebee
And her little honeys five.

"Buzz!" said the mother.
"We buzz," said the five.
And they buzzed all day
In the snug beehive.

Over in the meadow
In a nest built of sticks
Lived an old mother crow
And her little crows six.

"Caw!" said the mother.
"We caw," said the six.
And they cawed all day
In the nest made of sticks.

Over in the meadow
In a green grassy heaven
Lived an old mother spider
And her little spiders seven.

"Spin!" said the mother.
"We spin," said the seven.
And they spun rainbow webs
In the green grassy heaven.

Over in the meadow
Near the old garden gate
Lived an old mother lizard
And her little lizards eight.

"Bask!" said the mother.
"We bask," said the eight.
And they basked all day
On the old garden gate.

Over in the meadow
Where the clear pools shine
Lived an old mother frog
And her little froggies nine.

"Jump!" said the mother.
"We jump," said the nine.
And they jumped all night
Where the clear pools shine.

Over in the meadow
In the soft shady glen
Lived a mother firefly
And her fireflies ten.

"Shine!" said the mother.
"We shine," said the ten.
And they shone like stars
In the soft shady glen.

17

When my parents were kids, did they have to listen to what grown-ups told them to do?

Yes, they did. When your parents were kids, they had a mommy and daddy just like you. Their parents told them what to do. They told them when it was time to go to bed. They told them when it was time to clean up their rooms. Did they listen? You can ask your grandparents. Why? Because your parents' parents are your grandparents.

Why do I look like my parents?

What you look like depends on your genes. When you were first created from a tiny cell from your father and a tiny cell from your mother, your genes were in those cells. Genes are like a plan for what you will look like. The color of your hair and eyes, the shape of your nose, how tall you are, whether you have freckles or not all depend on your genes. Since the genes came from your parents, it makes sense that you look like them. But sometimes genes have surprises, and you can wind up looking like your great-grandmother or like no one else in your family!

18

Do animals have families just like ours?

Most animals take care of their young and help them grow. Mother and father birds bring food to their little ones in the nest. A baby hippopotamus lives with its mother in the water. It rides on her back when she swims in deep water. A mother bat hangs her baby upside down from a tree branch and goes out and hunts for food. But animal families with a mom and dad and kids living together are unusual. Beavers have families that are like ours. They live together in a shelter made out of sticks called a lodge. Each lodge has just one family in it: a mother, a father, children that are about a year old, and new babies.

When twins look exactly alike, do their parents ever get them mixed up?

Some twins look so much alike that it is very hard to tell them apart. But no two people are exactly alike. There are always ways that they look a little different. The better you get to know twins the easier it is to tell them apart. Parents know their children better than anyone—so they hardly ever get them confused. Some parents make it easier for people to tell their twins apart by cutting their hair in different styles—or by dressing them in different colors. Do you know any twins? How do you tell them apart?

19

I Hear My Mother's

soft voice reading
poems to me
words like music
over and over

I hear the sound
of her cooking spoon
beating against a white bowl
in her sweet-smelling kitchen

I hear her car
turning into
the driveway
home from work

I hear her heels taptapping
as she comes
into the bedroom
to kiss me good-night

and I feel
her smooth skin
as she takes me in her arms
and holds me tight

Ruth Whitman

My Father

My father is tall
and strong as a giant.
I bet
with his bare hands
he could break rocks in half.
But when I told him this one day,
he picked me up
and held me close
so that I *felt* his tenderness and
the rumble of his laugh.

Charlotte Zolotow

The Hurry-Up Family
by Cathy Dubowski

Wake up, sweetheart!"
Lauren opened her eyes as her mother pulled back the covers.

"It's too cold!" Lauren mumbled, holding on to the blanket.

"We've got to hurry," said Mom. "It's almost time to go!"

Lauren yawned and sat up. "Hurry and dress now," said Mom. "I've got an important meeting this morning—I *can't* be late!"

Lauren pulled on her clothes and hurried into the kitchen. Dad was knotting his tie and reading the newspaper while he waited for his toast to pop up. Lauren's big brother David was doing last-minute homework and listening to the radio as he ate a blueberry muffin. Mom poured Lauren a bowl of cereal, then went back to ironing her blouse in front of the morning news on TV.

Minutes later Mom was zipping up Lauren's coat. "Don't forget to

turn on the answering machine!"
Mom called to Dad. "And the
dishwasher and the washing
machine. And, David, turn off the
radio!"

Soon they were all bundled up and
out the door. Mom and Lauren got
in one car and drove off toward
Lauren's preschool and Mom's job.
Dad and David got in the other
car and drove off in the opposite
direction, toward David's school
and Dad's job.

"Another hurry-up day," thought
Lauren.

That night Lauren helped set the
table as Mom popped the dinner in
the microwave and read the mail.
Dad and David came in late. At last
they all sat down to eat. Mom talked
about the committee meeting she
had to get ready for. Dad talked about
a report he had to write. David
talked about his big basketball game
at school. Lauren played with her peas.

After all the lights were out that

night, Lauren slipped out of bed. She pulled back the curtains and pressed her nose against the cold windowpane. She wanted to make a wish. But there wasn't a single star in the sky. . . .

The next morning Lauren awoke with a start.

"Look at that!" cried Dad.

"What a surprise!" said Mom.

Lauren jumped out of bed and ran into the family room. Mom, Dad, and David were staring out the big picture window.

"Snow!" cried Lauren. The whole backyard was white. The sky was filled with a flurry of big, thick snowflakes.

They turned on the radio. ". . . Possible accumulation of ten to twelve inches," the newscaster said. All the schools and most offices

were closed.

"What about my meeting?!" cried Mom.

"What about my report?!" moaned Dad.

"What about my basketball game at school?!" groaned David.

Mom, Dad, and David did not look happy. Lauren was very happy!

"Come on!" shouted Lauren, jumping up and down. "No school! No work! Let's go play in the snow!"

Dad looked at Mom. Mom looked at David. Then they all laughed. "Good idea!" said Mom. "No reason to rush today!"

Soon the four of them were walking hand in hand in the snow. The snowflakes tickled as they landed on Lauren's cheeks. David showed Lauren a red cardinal in the snowy branches of a tree. Mom and Dad threw snowballs at each other, just like kids.

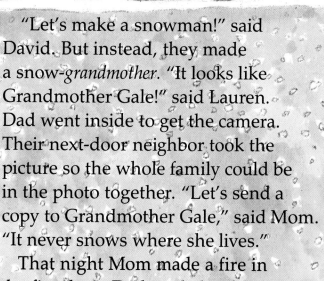

"Let's make a snowman!" said David. But instead, they made a snow-*grandmother*. "It looks like Grandmother Gale!" said Lauren. Dad went inside to get the camera. Their next-door neighbor took the picture so the whole family could be in the photo together. "Let's send a copy to Grandmother Gale," said Mom. "It never snows where she lives."

That night Mom made a fire in the fireplace. Dad made his famous homemade hot chocolate. The whole family worked on the letter to Grandmother Gale.

A week later they got a letter back from Grandmother Gale. It said, "Thanks for the picture. The snow-grandmother looks just like me, but you all look different—you're not in a big hurry!"

Lauren knew just what Grandmother Gale meant.

26

The Marvelous Toy

When I was just a wee little lad
Full of health and joy,
My father homeward came one night
And gave to me a toy.
A wonder to behold it was,
With many colors bright,
And the moment I laid eyes on it,
It became my heart's delight.

Chorus

It went "zip" when it moved
And "bop" when it stopped
And "whirr" when it stood still.
I never knew just what it was,
And I guess I never will.

The first time that I picked it up,
I had a big surprise,
For right on its bottom were two big buttons
That looked like big green eyes.
I first pushed one and then the other,
And then I twisted its lid,
And when I set it down again,
Here is what it did.

Chorus

28

It first marched left and then marched right,
And then marched under a chair,
And when I looked where it had gone,
It wasn't even there!
I started to sob and my daddy laughed,
For he knew that I would find,
When I turned around my marvelous toy
Chuggin' from behind.

Chorus

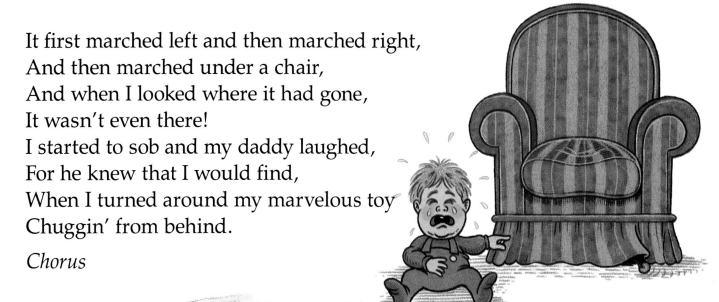

Well, the years have gone by too quickly it seems,
And I have my own little boy,
And yesterday I gave to him
My marv'lous little toy.
His eyes nearly popped right out of his head,
And he gave a squeal of glee.
Neither one of us knows just what it is,
But he loves it just like me.
It still goes "zip" when it moves
And "bop" when it stops
And "whirr" when it stands still.
I never knew just what it was,
And I guess I never will.

Tom Paxton

Kids

Why It Would Be Good to Have a Really Big Family

If I had twelve sisters
And thirty-one brothers,
When you got me mad
I could play with the others!

Jeff Moss

The Three Brothers

A Retelling of the Tale by the Brothers Grimm

Once upon a time there was an old man who had three sons, a fine house, and nothing else in the world. The old man loved his sons equally, so he couldn't decide which one should have the house when he died. At last he decided to sell the house and divide the money among his three sons.

But this made the boys very sad. "Please don't sell the house, Father," said the youngest. "We have all been so happy here. I would rather have this house than all the money in the world."

The older brothers felt the same way, so the old man did not sell the house. "But what will I do?" he asked.

"I have an idea," said the eldest son. "Each of us will go out into the world and learn a trade. In exactly one year we will come home and show you what we have learned. The brother who knows his trade the best will get the house."

"I suppose that's fair," said the old man.

The other brothers agreed. So the next day, the three boys went out into the world to learn a trade. The first brother found work as a blacksmith's apprentice. Soon he had learned his trade so well that the king himself hired him to shoe the royal horses.

The second brother became a barber. He was such a good barber that all the richest people in the kingdom would let no one else touch their hair.

The youngest son became a swordsman. He had a harder time than his brothers, for the kingdom was full of excellent swordsmen. But he was determined to be the best, and he refused to give up.

It was a busy year, and it passed quickly for the three boys. When it

was over, they all met at their father's house. He had missed them terribly, and was very happy to see them. To celebrate their homecoming, he set up an outdoor feast in the field behind the house.

The brothers ate to their heart's content. Then it was time to demonstrate their skills. But how? As they were thinking about this, a coach sped past, pulled by two galloping horses. As the horses dashed by, the first brother removed their horseshoes and put on new ones, without stopping the coach!

The old man was amazed. "My

eldest son is the fastest blacksmith in the kingdom! Surely he will have the house," he thought to himself.

But the second son was not to be outdone. Just then, a rabbit hopped into the field from the woods. The second brother quickly got his razor and shaving cream. He lathered up the rabbit's whiskers and shaved his chin clean as a whistle. And he did this while the rabbit raced past him at top speed!

"Oh, my!" thought the old man. "My second son is just as clever as my first son! They *both* deserve to have the house!"

Just then, a black cloud appeared overhead, and soon it began to rain. The old man was disappointed because their feast was spoiled. But the youngest son took out his sword and began to bat the raindrops away. *Ping ping ping!* The rain came down fast and hard, but not one drop touched the youngest son. The faster it rained, the faster the boy flashed his sword. All the others got wet, but the youngest son was as dry as if he were sitting under a roof.

"Incredible!" cried the old man. "My youngest son, you win the house!"

The older brothers agreed, and proudly clapped the youngest on the back. Then, because he loved his brothers so much, the youngest son invited them to live in the house with him. And live there they did, as happy as could be.

DO'S AND DON'TS FOR KIDS

DO give your mom a hug.

DON'T hug her right after you've been fingerpainting.

DO ask your dad to play ball.

DON'T ask him when he's washing the car.

DO put away all your toys when your parents tell you to.

DON'T put them away in your bed.

DO practice your exercises.

DON'T practice them on your dad.

The Twins

In form and feature, face and limb,
   I grew so like my brother,
That folks got taking me for him,
   And each for one another.
It puzzled all our kith and kin,
   It reached an awful pitch;
For one of us was born a twin,
   Yet not a soul knew which.

Henry S. Leigh

40

There are five sets of identical twins in this picture.
Can you find them all?
Identical twins are two people who look exactly alike.

41

Wait for William

by Marjorie Flack

nce there were three
children who lived
in a white house on
Pollywinkle Lane in the
village of Pleasantville.

The oldest of these three children
was a big boy whose name was
Charles and he was eight years old.

The middle one was a girl whose
name was Nancy and she was six
years old.

The youngest was a little boy and
his name was William and he was
just four years old.

One summer morning when
William was riding his scooter up
and down the walk Charles said,

"Hurry up, William, put away your
scooter and we will take you down
to Main Street to see the Circus
Parade."

And Nancy said, "Hurry up,
William, wash your hands and comb
your hair and we will take you down
to Main Street to see the Circus
Parade."

So William put away his scooter
and he washed his hands and combed
his hair, and they all started out
down Pollywinkle Lane on their way
to Main Street to see the Circus
Parade.

"Hurry up, William," said Charles.
"Walk faster, William. We must not

42

be too late when we get to Main Street to see the Circus Parade."

"Hurry up, William; walk faster, William," said Nancy, "or we shall be too late when we get to Main Street to see the Circus Parade."

William walked faster but Charles walked faster and Nancy walked faster as they all hurried along down Pollywinkle Lane on their way to Main Street to see the Circus Parade.

Then *flop*, off came William's shoe, and there he stood with one shoe off and one shoe on. "Wait for me!" called William. "Wait for me, my shoe's come off!"

But Charles and Nancy did not answer. They did not answer because they did not hear William. They did

not hear William because they were too far away, as they hurried along down Pollywinkle Lane on their way to Main Street to see the Circus Parade.

So William stopped and he put on his shoe and he tied the shoestring in a tight, firm knot, and then he slowly and carefully made the ends into a proper, neat bow.

But when it was all done Nancy and Charles were gone; they were nowhere in sight! So William ran alone. He ran all alone down Pollywinkle Lane on his way to Main Street to see the Circus Parade.

Then William stopped; he stopped at a corner because he heard music; William heard circus music coming nearer and nearer, and then William saw the Circus Parade coming to him, coming to William on its way to Main Street.

First came the horses—then came the band—and then the camels— and then came a man leading an elephant.

43

The man saw William. He saw William standing all alone, all alone because Charles and Nancy and everybody else, everybody else in the whole village of Pleasantville, had gone to Main Street to see the Circus Parade.

"Want a ride?" called the man.

"Yes!" said William.

So the man lifted William up, up high on the elephant, and William and the elephant paraded along to Main Street.

William was so high the branches of the trees were near him and he looked way down on all the people of Pleasantville as they stood on Main Street to see the Circus Parade!

William passed by the drugstore, he passed by the grocery store, and

he passed by the church, and then, when he came to the post office, William looked down, way down, and there he saw Charles and Nancy and all their friends!

Charles and Nancy and all their friends looked up, way up, and there on top of the elephant they saw William riding the elephant in the Circus Parade!

"Look at William!" shouted Charles.

"Look at William!" shouted Nancy.

"Look at William!" shouted all their friends.

Then they all ran along beside William as he rode the elephant in the Circus Parade.

They went up Summer Street, and then down High Street, and then they came to the corner of Pollywinkle Lane.

Then the man lifted William down. He lifted William down, down to the ground again.

"Thank you for the elephant ride," said William. The man said, "You're welcome." Then the man and the elephant went away.

"Tell us about it," begged Charles.

"Tell us about it," begged Nancy.

"Tell us about riding the elephant in the Circus Parade," begged all their friends.

But William said, "Wait. Wait. My other shoe is untied."

So Charles waited, and Nancy waited, and all their friends waited, while William tied the shoestring in a good, firm knot, and they waited while he slowly and carefully made the ends into a proper, neat bow.

Then slowly they walked, walked slowly with William as he told them about riding the elephant down Main Street, down Main Street in the Circus Parade.

46

Luck

I didn't come out of my mother.
I don't have my father's green eyes.
No one in the family looks like me.
People are always surprised.

I think we're a happier family
Than if we were all kings and queens.
We're so lucky we all found each other.
That's what being adopted means.

Pamela Espeland and Marilyn Waniek

47

Ten in a Bed

**Here's a song that's fun to sing and a game that's fun to play!
Just look at the little pictures, and they'll tell you what to do
with your hand.**

There were ten in the bed, and the little one said,

"Roll over, roll over."

So they all rolled over and one fell out.

There were nine in the bed, and the little one said,

"Roll over, roll over."

So they all rolled over and one fell out.

There were eight in the bed, and the little one said,

"Roll over, roll over."

So they all rolled over and one fell out.

There were seven in the bed, and the little one said,

"Roll over, roll over."

So they all rolled over and one fell out.

There were six in the bed,  and the little one said,

"Roll over, roll over."

So they all rolled over and one fell out.

There were five in the bed, and the little one said,

"Roll over, roll over."

So they all rolled over and one fell out.

There were four in the bed, and the little one said,

"Roll over, roll over."

So they all rolled over and one fell out.

There were three in the bed, and the little one said,

"Roll over, roll over."

So they all rolled over and one fell out.

There were two in the bed, and the little one said,

"Roll over, roll over."

So they all rolled over and one fell out.

There was one in the bed, and the little one said,

"Good night!"

A Family Together

My Family

Part of my family is grown-up and tall.
Part of my family is little and small.
I'm in the middle and pleased with them all.

Marchette Chute

The Family McFee

Katie McFee has a big family,
About as big as a family can be.
Katie has a father and also a mother,
   two grandmas,
   two grandpas,
   three sisters,
   one brother,
and almost too many uncles to name, plus a
whole lot of aunts who look sort of the same.

   There's Uncle Sam and Uncle Lou,
   Judd, Jed, and Jeffrey, to name just a few.
   The twins are Uncles Dan and Stan.
   The lady in green is Auntie Jan.
   Aunt Gladys is whispering to Uncle Fred.
   Aunt Hortense is dancing with Uncle Ted.
   Uncle Bill walks with a cane.
   Aunt Jill came prepared for rain.
   Uncle Roy just joined the Navy.
   Oops! Aunt Joy just spilled the gravy.

There are dozens of cousins, from Agnes to Zack.
But the one Kate loves best is sweet baby Jack.
   The one with the kitty is cousin Belinda.
   The one who's so pretty is cousin Melinda.
   Cousin Joe's fast asleep in Dad's easy chair.
   Cousin Glo's cuddled up with her favorite bear.
   Cousin Mo's putting gum in his cousin Bo's hair...
   Kate's cousins are here, there, and everywhere.

But where is dear Katie? She seems to be missing...
To find her, just look for the one Bo is kissing!

Teddy Slater

52

Look at the picture and find Katie McFee's cousins, aunts, and uncles.

ALL ABOUT ME AND MY FAMILY

by Cathy Dubowski

This story is all about you and your family! Read the sentences, then point to the picture that tells what's true about you and your family. Or if you want, point to the pictures that make a silly story.

This is a story about my family.

This is how many people are in my family—including *me*:

1 2 3 4 5 6 7 8 300

We live in a

I have a brother or sister who likes to

54

Our family likes to eat

On our vacation, my family likes to go to

My father's job is

My mother's job is

My job is

My family likes to share

My aunt is very good at

One time my uncle

56

The cousin who lives closest to me is

When I visit my grandmother's house, we like to bake

My grandfather almost always wears a

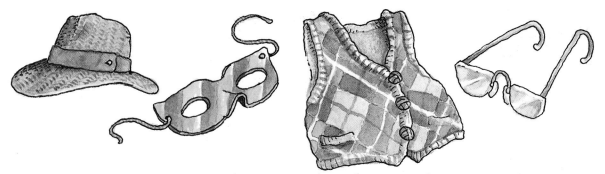

When I think about my family, it makes me

Afternoon With Grandmother

I always shout when Grandma comes,
But Mother says, "Now please be still
And good and do what Grandma wants."
And I say, "Yes, I will."

So off we go in Grandma's car.
"There's a brand-new movie quite near by,"
She says, "that I'd rather like to see."
And I say, "So would I."

The show has horses and chases and battles;
We gasp and hold hands the whole way through.
She smiles and says, "I liked that lots."
And I say, "I did, too."

"It's made me hungry, though," she says,
"I'd like a malt and tarts with jam.
By any chance are you hungry, too?"
And I say, "Yes, I am."

Later at home my mother says,
"I hope you were careful to do as bid.
Did you and Grandma have a good time?"
And I say, "YES, WE DID!!!"

Barbara A. Huff

58

Grandpa Dropped
His Glasses

Grandpa dropped his glasses once
In a pot of dye,
And when he put them on again
He saw a purple sky.
Purple birds were rising up
From a purple hill,
Men were grinding purple cider
At a purple mill.
Purple Adeline was playing
With a purple doll,
Little purple dragonflies
Were crawling up the wall.
And at the supper table
He got crazy as a loon
From eating purple apple dumplings
With a purple spoon.

Leroy F. Jackson

Here Comes a Baby

by Margaret Wise Brown

he bunnies were expecting a baby.

"When will it be here?" asked the three little Bunnies.

"When it comes," said the Mother Bunny.

The three little Bunnies ran to the window to see if the baby was coming.

But they couldn't see it. Not there. Though one Bunny said he could see it on a cloud in the air.

Whose baby Bunny will it be?

"Here comes a baby," cried the fat little Bunny. "He's still far away but he looks rather funny. A little old baby as blind as a mole. Do you think there's room for another in our hole?"

"No room, no room," squealed the three little Bunnies.

"No," said the fat Bunny. "Not where I live. I don't want a baby and I'll pull its whiskers when it gets here."

"I'll sit on it if it sits in my chair," said the littlest Bunny, who really had a little chair.

"It could live in the garden," said the middle-sized Bunny. "It doesn't look very big."

The baby was always coming nearer. And, of course, they couldn't

see it, but they pretended they could. And it came nearer and nearer.

"I'll sew it some clothes," said the Mother Bunny. "The clothes won't be very big."

"I'll make it a bed," said the Father Bunny. "The bed won't be very big."

"I'll pick it some flowers," said the fat little Bunny. "Little tiny flowers because its nose won't be very big."

"I'll build it a hat," said the middle-sized Bunny. "The hat doesn't have

to be big."

The littlest Bunny didn't say a thing.

As they thought about it, the baby grew larger and the time for it to come was almost here.

"Here comes a baby," cried the little fat Bunny. "It can't sleep in my bed. There isn't room here for anyone but me."

"It can't have my blocks," said the middle-sized Bunny. "It can't play in my cabbage garden."

"It's very little," said the littlest Bunny. "We could find it a little acorn to play with."

"Here it comes, here it comes," cried the Father Bunny.

"Here it is," said the Mother Bunny. "It has hair and toes and eyes and nose and eyelashes."

"It's mine, it's mine," squealed the three little Bunnies.

"It can sleep in my bed," said the little fat Bunny.

"It can sit in my chair," said the littlest Bunny.

"But it can't be me," squealed the middle-sized Bunny. "But I'll give it the tiny flowers."

"It's mine, it's mine," cried the Mother Bunny.

"It's thine and mine," said the Father Bunny.

"It's ours," cried the whole Bunny family.

Little People™ Big Book About FAMILIES

TIME-LIFE for CHILDREN™

Publisher: Robert H. Smith
Managing Editor: Neil Kagan
Associate Editors: Jean Burke Crawford
Patricia Daniels
Marketing Director: Ruth P. Stevens
Promotion Director: Kathleen B. Tresnak
Associate Promotion Director: Jane B. Welihozkiy
Production Manager: Prudence G. Harris
Editorial Consultants: Jacqueline A. Ball
Sara Mark

PRODUCED BY PARACHUTE PRESS, INC.

Editorial Designer: Joan Waricha
Editors: Ann Hardy, Christopher Medina,
Jane Stine, Wendy Wax
Writers: Cathy East Dubowski, H.L. Ross,
Teddy Slater, Natalie Standiford
Designer: Lillian Lovitt
Illustrators: R.W. Alley (pp. 54-57), Pat & Robin
DeWitt (pp. 12-17), Dennis Hockerman
(pp. 4-9, 58-59), Terry Kovalcik (pp.
18-19, 38-39), Loretta Krupinski (pp.
20-21, 47), Allan Neuwirth (pp. 28-29,
48-49), Dana Regan (pp. 40-41), Gill
Speirs (endpapers), John Speirs (cover,
pp. 2-3, 10-11, 22-27, 30-31, 42-46, 50-51,
52-53), Jody Wheeler (pp. 32-37), Tad Zar
(pp. 60-63)

Fourth printing 1992. Printed in U.S.A.
Published simultaneously in Canada.

Time-Life Books Inc. is a wholly owned subsidiary of THE TIME INC. BOOK COMPANY.

TIME-LIFE is a trademark of Time Warner Inc. U.S.A.

FISHER-PRICE, LITTLE PEOPLE and AWNING DESIGN are trademarks of Fisher-Price, Division of The Quaker Oats Company, and are used under license.

Time-Life Books Inc. offers a wide range of fine publications, including home video products. For subscription information, call 1-800-621-7026 or write TIME-LIFE BOOKS, P.O. Box C-32068, Richmond, Virginia 23261-2068.

ACKNOWLEDGMENTS

Every effort has been made to trace the ownership of all copyrighted material and to secure the necessary permissions to reprint these selections. If any question arises as to the use of any material, the editor and the publisher, while expressing regret for any inadvertent error, will make the necessary correction in future printings.

Grateful acknowledgment is made to the following for permission to reprint copyrighted material: Bantam Books (a division of Bantam Doubleday Dell) for "Why It Would Be Good to Have a Really Big Family" from THE BUTTERFLY JAR by Jeff Moss. Copyright © 1989 by Jeff Moss. Carolrhoda Books for "Luck" from THE CAT WALKED THROUGH THE CASSEROLE by Pamela Espeland and Marilyn Waniek. Copyright © 1984 by Pamela Espeland and Marilyn Waniek. Cherry Lane Music Publishing Co., Inc. for THE MARVELOUS TOY by Tom Paxton. Copyright © 1961, 1964 by Cherry Lane Music Publishing Co., Inc. Harcourt Brace Jovanovich for "My Father" from EVERYTHING GLISTENS AND EVERYTHING SINGS by Charlotte Zolotow. Copyright © 1967 by Charlotte Zolotow. Harper & Row for "Andre" from THE BRONZEVILLE BOYS AND GIRLS by Gwendolyn Brooks. Copyright © 1956 by Gwendolyn Brooks Blakely; and "Under the Sunday Tree" from UNDER THE SUNDAY TREE by Eloise Greenfield. Copyright © 1988 by Eloise Greenfield. Barbara Huff for "Afternoon With Grandmother." Robert C. Jackson for "Grandpa Dropped His Glasses" by Leroy Jackson. Harold Ober Associates Inc. for WAIT FOR WILLIAM by Marjorie Flack. Copyright © 1935 by Marjorie Flack Larsson, renewed 1963 by Hilma Larsson Barnum. Mary Chute Smith for "My Family" from RHYMES ABOUT US by Marchette Chute. Copyright © 1974 by E.P. Dutton. Western Publishing Co. for "Here Comes a Baby" from THE GOLDEN BUNNY by Margaret Wise Brown. Copyright © 1953 by Western Publishing Co. Ruth Whitman for "I Hear My Mother's."

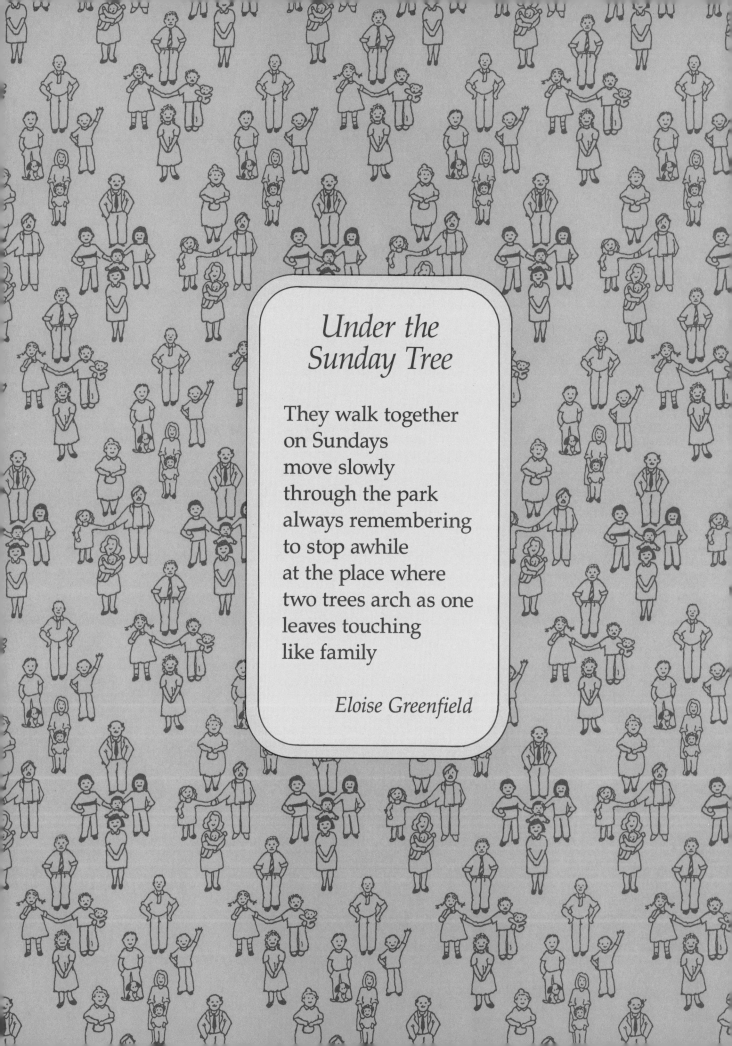

Under the Sunday Tree

They walk together
on Sundays
move slowly
through the park
always remembering
to stop awhile
at the place where
two trees arch as one
leaves touching
like family

Eloise Greenfield